SHAPED BY SCRIPTURE

In Him Was Life

JOHN

JEREN ROWELL

Contents

3

THE *SHAPED BY SCRIPTURE* SERIES

The first step of an organized study of the Bible is the selection of a biblical book, which is not always an easy task. Often people pick a book they are already familiar with, books they think will be easy to understand, or books that, according to popular opinion, seem to have more relevance to Christians today than other books of the Bible. However, it is important to recognize the truth that God's Word is not limited to just a few books. All the biblical books, both individually and collectively, communicate God's Word to us. As Paul affirms in 2 Timothy 3:16, "All Scripture is God-breathed and is useful for teaching, rebuking, correcting and training in righteousness." We interpret the term "God-breathed" to mean inspired by God. If Christians are going to take 2 Timothy 3:16 seriously, then we should all set the goal of encountering God's Word as communicated through all sixty-six books of the Bible. New Christians or those with little to no prior knowledge of the Bible might find it best to start with a New Testament book like 1 John, James, or one of the four Gospels (Matthew, Mark, Luke, or John).

By purchasing this volume, you have chosen to study the Gospel of John. You have made a great choice because this Gospel is less a historical recounting of Jesus's life and ministry (though these features are certainly present) and more a theological narrative that connects the story of Jesus with the grand story of God. In other words, John recounts what God has done through Jesus Christ to redeem creation, especially his children—us! The goal of this series is to illustrate an appropriate method for studying the Bible, so instead of a comprehensive study of the book of John, this volume will be limited to a few select passages from the Gospel that have been chosen as foundational and representative of the story John means to tell and his reason for telling it.

How This Study Works

This Bible study is intended for a period of seven weeks. We have chosen a specific passage for each week's study. This study can be done individually or with a small group.

For individual study, we recommend a five-day study each week, following the guidelines given below:

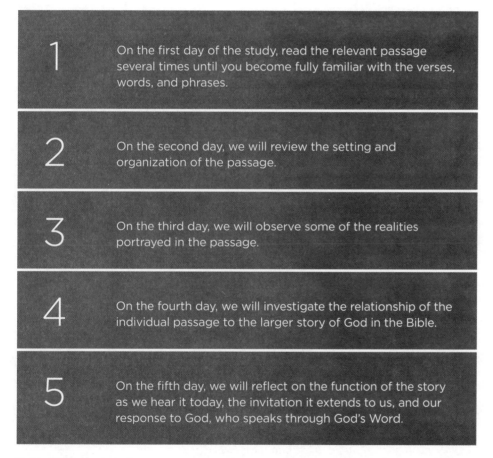

1   On the first day of the study, read the relevant passage several times until you become fully familiar with the verses, words, and phrases.

2   On the second day, we will review the setting and organization of the passage.

3   On the third day, we will observe some of the realities portrayed in the passage.

4   On the fourth day, we will investigate the relationship of the individual passage to the larger story of God in the Bible.

5   On the fifth day, we will reflect on the function of the story as we hear it today, the invitation it extends to us, and our response to God, who speaks through God's Word.

If this Bible study is done as a group activity, we recommend that members of the group meet together on the sixth day to share and discuss what they have learned from God's Word and how it has transformed their lives.

You may want to have a study Bible to give you additional insights as we work through the book of John. Other helpful resources are *Discovering the New Testament* and the *New Beacon Bible Commentaries John 1-12* and *John 13-21*, available from The Foundry Publishing.

6.

Literary Forms in the Bible

There are several literary forms represented throughout the Bible. The divinely inspired writers used various techniques to communicate God's Word to their ancient audiences. The major literary forms (also known as genres) of the Bible are:

- narratives

- laws

- history

- Wisdom literature (in the form of dialogues and proverbial statements)

- poetry (consisting of poems of praise, lament, trust in God, and more)

- prophecy

- discourses

- parables

- miracle stories

- letters (also known as epistles)

- exhortations

- apocalyptic writings

Within each of these forms, one may find subgenres. Each volume in the *Shaped by Scripture* series will briefly overview the genres found in the book of the Bible that is the subject of that study.

When biblical writers utilized a particular literary form, they intended for it to have a specific effect on their audience. This concept can be understood by examining genres that are familiar to us in our contemporary setting. For example, novels that are comedies inspire good and happy feelings in their readers; tragedies, on the other hand, are meant to induce sorrow. What is true of the intended effect of literary forms in contemporary literature is also true of literary forms found in the Bible.

THE BOOK OF JOHN

The message of the biblical books, though it originates with God, comes to us through individuals whom God inspired to communicate his word to humanity. They fulfilled their task by utilizing their literary skill as speakers and writers of God's message. This message came to these individuals in particular circumstances in the history of God's people—the Israelites in the Old Testament period, and the Christian church in the first century AD. In addition, biblical books communicate certain clearly developed understandings about God, humanity, sin, judgment, salvation, human hope, and more. Bible studies should be done with an awareness of the theological themes in a particular book. So, prior to our engagement with the actual text of John, we will briefly summarize what we know about the book in general, the authorship of John, literary forms found in the book, the historical setting of the book and that of its writing, and its major theological themes.

Unique among the Gospels

John's distinctiveness in its genre is evident from the start. Unlike the Gospels of Matthew and Luke, which begin their stories with Jesus's family, location, and birth, and unlike the Gospel of Mark, which begins with Jesus's baptism, the Gospel of John begins with theology. "In the beginning was the Word" (1:1) signals to us that John is doing something special in his telling of Jesus's story. John means to help us understand how the embodied revelation of God in Jesus is the center point of all history and the organizing logic of the entire story of God. Christians often refer to the Bible as "the Word of God," and this is fine and true. However, John helps us remember that the Word of God is first and foremost the second person of the Trinity. John is talking about the One who "made his dwelling among us" (1:14) and who was "with God in the beginning" (1:2). Most essentially, the Word of God is Jesus Christ the Lord, and the Bible faithfully tells us the story of our redemption in Christ Jesus. This new life is the focal point of John's Gospel narrative.

Who Wrote John?

The answer to this may seem obvious since the book is called "Gospel of John" or "The Gospel according to John." But actually, there is no author named anywhere in the book. Still, the early church connected this Gospel with the apostle John. One of the interesting features of this Gospel is the repetition of the phrase "the disciple whom Jesus loved." While this person is never explicitly identified, the references suggest that the Gospel is the author's first-person account. Scholars have long studied the authorship of this Gospel and have arrived at a number of both certain and uncertain conclusions about the identity of its author. What we do know for sure is that the author understood himself to be a witness to Jesus's life and ministry and viewed it as his sacred duty to bear witness to these things. Clearly, John is writing more than a chronological account of Jesus's life—he is proclaiming the good news that "God so loved the world that he gave his one and only Son, that whoever believes in him shall not perish but have eternal life" (3:16).

Literary Form

Whereas the Synoptic Gospels (Matthew, Mark, and Luke) center on Jesus's teaching and miracles, John focuses more on interactions that come in the form of discussions, dialogues, and long speeches. John doesn't feature parables and sayings in the same way the Synoptic Gospels do; in John, Jesus never says, "The kingdom of God is like . . ."

Another interesting and important feature is the author's commentary and explanatory notes. For example, in the story of Jesus's encounter with a Samaritan woman in chapter 4, John inserts a number of comments, including an explanation that "Jews do not associate with Samaritans." This note, and others like it, indicate the author's personal engagement with the narrative as a witness to its events as well as the author's understanding that he was writing to an audience that included gentiles.

Entering the Story

The Gospel of John is a rich text that is alive with stories of inspiration, challenge, and encouragement. The Holy Spirit continues to speak to the church through this Gospel by helping us see Jesus in his glory as the crucified and risen Lord. John is best read as a story that paints a compelling portrait of the One who is life (1:4), light (1:5), living water (4:14), bread of life (6:35), and more. Perhaps this is why "not-yet" believers and new believers are often encouraged to use John as a starting point in their Bible reading—John's narrative focuses on Jesus in conversation with people.

Great teachers practice the art of asking good questions. Teachers certainly provide content, but the best teachers understand their task as more than giving information. Impactful teachers know that the best learning comes from wrestling with our own deep questions—the kind of questions they know how to spark by asking their own good questions.

Jesus was a master at the art of asking questions. We see this throughout all the Gospels, but John especially seems to use the questions that Jesus posed to people as a way of organizing definitive interactions with a wide variety of people throughout the narrative. We find at least two dozen questions in John, sometimes spoken to crowds but often posed directly to people in one-on-one conversation. For example, Jesus asked John's disciples who began to follow him, "What do you want?" (1:38). He asked a lame man, "Do you want to get well?" (5:6). And he asked Peter, "Do you love me?" (21:16).

It is fascinating and instructive to trace these questions of Jesus in the Gospel of John, which can be unsettling and disturbing, or they can also be comforting and healing. John is giving us a way to see Jesus that at once demonstrates his full humanity yet also reveals his full divinity. John shows us that when we see Jesus, we see more than a compassionate healer and wise teacher—we see God (14:9). John gives us these stories under the inspiration of the Holy Spirit so that we might "believe that Jesus is the Messiah," and that this faith might open us to the joy of "life in his name" (20:31).

Historical Context

If we are to faithfully read a text, it is important to know the time and location in which it was composed. Historical context helps us make sense of some of the references and movements in the story. For example, knowing that John is writing in the cultural convergence of Judaism (Hebrew culture) and Hellenism (Greek culture) is an important interpretive tool as we read the Gospel. This way, we can read through the lens of the tensions that exist between Jews and Gentiles as they come together in the way of Jesus. We get a vivid picture of these tensions in Acts, particularly in chapter 15, when Paul and Barnabas are sent to Jerusalem to help church leaders achieve unity in the midst of their differences. John highlights another aspect of these tensions when he notes at least three times that Jewish believers are being "put out of the synagogue" (9:22, 12:42, 16:2)—a practice that leads some Jewish believers to keep their faith in Jesus a secret. This context helps us understand and perhaps empathize with characters like Nicodemus and Joseph of Arimathea, who find themselves caught between their religious standing and their belief in Jesus as Messiah.

Considering John's location may also help us understand some of the particular language he uses to tell his story. Throughout the Gospel, John takes a familiar language (Greek) and infuses some words with theological meaning in light of the revelation of God in Christ. For example, in what is usually called John's prologue (1:1–18), his use of the word *logos* is loaded with interpretive possibilities. With this word, John signals that he is reaching not only into the story of God's covenant people, Israel, to give the reason and rationale for the coming of the Messiah but also to the depths of creation and beyond to establish the preexistence of the one who now comes "full of grace and truth" (1:14). When Greek thinkers and philosophers used the term *logos*, it carried various possible meanings, including *reason, wisdom, speech, word, logic,* and more. John uses it to express the connection between God's divine, ordering logic that brought all of creation into existence, and the embodied revelation of God in the person of Jesus, the Word. We see this kind of play with poetic and theological language throughout John's Gospel.

In terms of the date of composition, most scholars agree that John was written after the three other New Testament Gospels, dating the writing somewhere between AD 80–95. It is evident from extrabiblical sources that this Gospel was known and referenced by the beginning of the second century. John's book is clearly different from those of Matthew, Mark, and Luke, which are often referred to as the Synoptic Gospels (*synoptic* means "seen together"). This term reflects the fact that first the three gospels share much in terms of content and structure, but they are written from different perspectives and for different audiences. They seem to have a common source in oral tradition and perhaps also a document that is no longer available to us. Additionally, each of their accounts spans about a one-year period. Conversely, John uses a unique structure in order to maximize his theological themes, and his account appears to span two to three years.

Structure and Organization

Many scholars have divided John into two movements: first, signs throughout Jesus's ministry that demonstrate his identity as the Son of God; and second, Jesus's purposeful movements toward and his experience of the Passion (his suffering and crucifixion), which ultimately shows his glory as the crucified and risen Savior. Following this structure, many scholars read John's Gospel as a twofold Book of Signs (chapters 1–12) and Book of Glory (chapters 13–20), with chapter 21 as an addition or appendix to the narrative. We might say that the turning point in the narrative is 13:1, in which John writes, "Jesus knew that the hour had come for him to leave this world and go to the Father."

Major Theological Themes

Our study of John will center in seven key themes that provide a theological structure for the study of the Gospel. Although we will narrow our focus to seven (fairly lengthy) passages, these seven signposts can help one to navigate the whole Gospel of John in a meaningful way.

There are several key theological themes at work in John:

 Jesus is fully divine and fully human. Jesus is God speaking to us, which is why John speaks of Jesus as the Word (1:1–18).

 Jesus helps us emerge from darkness, face the truth about ourselves, and discover new birth that brings everlasting life (3:1–21).

 Jesus is the bread from heaven that gives life to the world. Unlike physical bread that ultimately leaves us hungry again, the bread of life that is Jesus nourishes us for eternity (6:25–59).

 Jesus is the light of the world. He was sent by the Father into the darkness of a broken world to show us how to walk in the light that brings life (8:12–59).

 Jesus is the resurrection and the life. He not only becomes the firstfruits of resurrection, but he is also the very energy of redemption and new creation (11:1–44).

 The Holy Spirit is the gift of the Father, promised by Jesus, who becomes our Helper, Advocate, and Guide (chapters 14–17).

 Spirit-empowered believers are sent into the world to proclaim the good news of God's reconciling love (20:19–21:25).

JOHN 1

As we discussed in the introduction to this study, John's approach to telling the story of Jesus is different from that of Matthew, Mark, or Luke. John's uniqueness among the Gospels quickly becomes evident in our reading. In Genesis 1:1, the entire story begins with, "In the beginning God created the heavens and the earth." John 1:1 purposefully alludes to this language by starting with, "In the beginning was the Word."

Most translations divide the first chapter of John into three or four scenes, or movements. A simple way to outline the chapter is:

1. Prologue (1:1–18)

2. John's Testimony Regarding Jesus (1:19–34)

3. The First Disciples Are Called (1:35–51)

WEEK 1, DAY 1

Listen to the story in John 1 by reading it aloud several times until you become familiar with its verses, words, and phrases. Enjoy the experience of imagining the story in your mind, picturing each event as it unfolds.

WEEK 1, DAY 2

JOHN 1

The Setting

John begins by taking us back to before the beginning of the world. Before we are ever given the name "Jesus Christ" for the subject of this story, John takes us back to the presence of the Word who spoke creation into existence. In our Gospel, the author says that John (the baptizer) testified about "that light" (1:7) who is the Word. This introduces two themes—"light" and "life"—that are very important throughout the Gospel of John. In verse 17, the Baptist identifies the light explicitly as Jesus.

Later, we see that a group of priests and Levites (a particular class of priests) are sent to determine John's identity in light of the expected Messiah. It is important for the writer of this Gospel to deal explicitly with John the Baptist's identity before turning to establish the identity of Jesus, which is the central point of the Gospel. From this point, John the Baptist continues to testify about Jesus and introduce him to the first disciples.

The Plot

To discover the plot of John 1, let's divide the passage into ten sections. Below, summarize or paraphrase the general message or theme of each grouping of verses (following the pattern provided for verses 1–5, 6–8, and 47–51).

1. John 1:1–5

John begins by taking us back to "the Word"–the one who spoke creation into existence.

_____

_____

_____

2. John 1:6–8

God sent John the Baptist to testify about the light so that people might believe.

_____

_____

_____

3. John 1:9–13

_____

_____

_____

_____

_____

4. John 1:14–18

_____

_____

_____

_____

_____

5. John 1:19–23

_____

_____

_____

_____

_____

6. John 1:24–28

_____

_____

_____

_____

_____

7. John 1:29–34

_____

_____

_____

_____

_____

_____

8. John 1:35–39

_____

_____

_____

_____

_____

_____

9. John 1:40–46

_____

_____

_____

_____

_____

10. John 1:47–51

Jesus knew Nathanael before Nathanael was even aware of Jesus. Nathanael is amazed by

this, but Jesus says he will see greater things that are yet to come

_____

_____

_____

_____

What's Happening in the Story?

As we notice certain circumstances in the story, we will begin to see how they are similar to or different from the realities of our world. The story will become the lens through which we see the world in which we live today. In our study today, you may encounter words and/or phrases that are unfamiliar to you. Some of the particular words and translation choices for them have been explained in more detail in the **Word Study Notes**. If you are interested in even more help or detail, you can supplement this study with a Bible dictionary or other Bible study resource.

WORD STUDY NOTES #1

[1] As we will see throughout our study, "light" and "life" are very important words and ideas throughout the Gospel of John.

18

WORD STUDY NOTES #2

[1] We know from Luke's Gospel that John the Baptist and Jesus were related through their mothers, Elizabeth and Mary (Luke 1:36).

[2] John's role in "preparing the way" for Jesus as the long-awaited Messiah is a significant feature in the opening of all four Gospels.

1. John 1:1–5

John begins by identifying Jesus as "the Word." Our God is a God who speaks, and the Word spoke creation into existence. Here, the writer of the Gospel says that the Word (whom we know to be Jesus) is one in whom there is *life* and that this life is the *light* of all humankind.[1]

2. John 1:6–8

We are introduced to John, who is not the author of this Gospel but the one we have come to call "John the Baptist."[1] Here, the author says that God sent John the Baptist to testify about the light, who is the Word, so that people might believe.[2]

3. John 1:9–13

These verses point out that people may or may not acknowledge Jesus as the one who is life and light. As John says, even "his own did not receive him."

_____

_____

_____

4. John 1:14-18

In Jesus, we see the fullness of both grace and truth. These verses contain a central affirmation of the Christian faith: that God became human in the person of Jesus of Nazareth. John says that even though we have not seen God, Jesus is the one who makes God known to us.

5. John 1:19-23

John the Baptist is interrogated by priests and Levites who were sent by "the Jews."[1] John wants to make it clear that he does not claim to be the awaited Messiah.[2] The priests do not ask him, but John is able to anticipate the real interests of those who sent them by declaring, "I am not"—not the Christ, not Elijah, not the prophet.[3] Having established who John is not, the questioners now need something to take back to those who sent them, so they ask who he is. John answers by quoting the prophet Isaiah.

Practice the above pattern to summarize the world and reality that are portrayed in verses 24–28, 29–34, 35–42, and 43–46.

6. John 1:24-28

_____
_____
_____
_____
_____
_____
_____
_____
_____
_____
_____
_____
_____

WORD STUDY NOTES #5

[1] This phrase, "the Jews," comes up often in the Gospel with varied meaning. Usually, as in this case, it seems to refer to the Jewish religious officials in Jerusalem.

[2] The words John uses are *ego ouk eimi*: "I am not." Notably, in several places in John's Gospel, Jesus will use the words *ego eimi*: "I am" (followed by a predicate such as the bread of life, the light of the world, the good shepherd, etc.).

[3] John's response alerts us to the seriousness of this interrogation. The word translated as "testimony" in verse 19 is *marturia*, from which we get the English word "martyr." Sometimes it is translated as "witness."

WORD STUDY NOTES #7

[1] "The next day" could refer to either the day after John's interrogation by the religious officials or the day after the baptism of Jesus, which John does not explicitly recount here. Rather, he references it in verse 32 with a description that corresponds to the Synoptic versions of Jesus's baptism.

[2] John's "Lamb of God" language may come from Isaiah's vision of a suffering servant (Isaiah 53:7), or he may be remembering how his people escaped Egyptian slavery under the protection of lamb's blood on the doorposts. Both allusions may be involved, but it is also significant that this lamb "takes away the sin of the world." The word "sin" here is singular and would seem to have in view the general condition of a fallen world as well as the sins of individuals.

WORD STUDY NOTES #8

[1] The renaming of Simon right at the beginning of the narrative is unique to John. John may give us this story up front to highlight Jesus's foreknowledge, which is also displayed in the dialogue with Nathanael (1:47–51).

7. John 1:29–34[1, 2]

_____

_____

_____

_____

_____

_____

_____

_____

_____

_____

_____

8. John 1:35–42[1]

_____

_____

_____

_____

_____

_____

_____

_____

_____

_____

_____

_____

_____

9. John 1:43–46

_____
_____
_____
_____
_____
_____
_____
_____
_____
_____
_____

10. John 1:47–51

Jesus begins by praising Nathanael's faithfulness. His words obviously strike Nathanael as true because he asks how Jesus knows him. Jesus reveals that he saw Nathanael under the fig tree before Philip even fetched him.[1] Nathanael responds with a declaration of faith that Jesus is the Son of God. Jesus replies that Nathanael will see greater things than this — specifically, heavenly signs involving the Son of Man.[2]

_____
_____
_____
_____
_____
_____
_____
_____

WORD STUDY NOTES #10

[1] One interpretation of Jesus's allusion to the fig tree notes that it was common practice for rabbis to teach under fig trees—thus, the tree may allude to Nathanael's status as a learned person.

[2] The language of verse 51 may allude to Old Testament images of Jacob's "stairway to heaven" dream in Genesis 28 and Daniel's vision of the Son of Man's descent (Daniel 7:13). John may be bringing all of the claims of chapter 1 together in this verse to suggest that heaven and earth, humanity and the divine, meet in Jesus.

Discoveries

Let's summarize some of our discoveries from John 1.

1. Jesus is the Word who existed from the very beginning with God and always was God.

2. Our God is a God who speaks, and in the Gospel of John, we hear him through the Word who spoke creation into existence — Jesus.

3. God sent John the Baptist to prepare the way for the Messiah. When Jesus began his ministry, John did not claim to be the Messiah but instead testified that Jesus was God's chosen one.

4. The Word became flesh and lived among humanity as one of us. The incarnate Word (Jesus) is the Son who makes the Father fully known to us.

5. When Jesus called his first disciples, they immediately left behind what they knew and followed him. Moreover, they immediately embraced the evangelistic task of introducing others to him.

6. A natural response to meeting Jesus is to invite others we care about to "come and see," just as Andrew invited Peter and Philip invited Nathanael.

7. Just as Jesus knew Nathanael before Nathanael ever met him, he knows and understands us completely.

WEEK 1, DAY 4

John and the Story of God

If you have a study Bible, it may have references to other biblical texts in the margin, in a middle column, or in footnotes. As we seek to understand how the whole story of God ties together, you may find it helpful to reference some of those other scriptures from time to time. Whenever we read a biblical text, it is important to ask how it relates to the rest of the Bible.

In the space given below, write a short summary of how the theme of God knowing and speaking to humanity appears in each passage.

1. Exodus 33:9–11

The Exodus narrative gives us a vibrant picture of God and Moses

in fellowship and communication with one another. It is not one way,

but true dialogue.

_____

_____

_____

_____

_____

2. Psalm 99:6–7

_____

_____

_____

_____

_____

_____

_____

If you have a study Bible, it may have references in a margin, a middle column, or footnotes that point to other biblical texts. You may find it helpful in understanding how the whole story of God ties together to look up some of those other scriptures from time to time.

23

3. Isaiah 53:7

_____

_____

_____

_____

_____

_____

_____

_____

_____

4. Jeremiah 33:3

_____

_____

_____

_____

_____

_____

_____

5. Ezekiel 2:2

_____

_____

_____

_____

_____

_____

_____

_____

6. John 10:27–28

7. Hebrews 1:1–2

The author of Hebrews confirms that God has spoken to us through many different people and in many different ways throughout history, and now, God has spoken to us authoritatively through his own Son.

25

WEEK 1, DAY 5

John and Our World Today

When we enter into the intriguing narrative of John 1, the story becomes the lens through which we see ourselves, our world, and God's action in our world today.

1. What does it mean to us today to know that our God speaks to us?

It means that the story of God is not just part of church history—rather, God actively reveals himself in our lives today. Just as the disciples and Nathanael had to decide how to react to Jesus when they met him, we too have a responsibility to respond to God when he reveals himself to us.

Following the above example, answer these questions about how we understand ourselves, our world, and God's action in our world today.

2. Who in your life testified to the light of Jesus? What does this say to you about your own opportunity to bear witness about the light?

3. What do you think the first disciples saw, heard, or felt in their interaction with Jesus that inspired them to leave their old lives behind and immediately follow him? What is it about your knowledge of Jesus that inspires your faith?

4. How do you feel about the fact that Jesus knows everything about you? What areas of your life might you be tempted to think you are hiding from him?

_____

_____

_____

_____

_____

Invitation and Response

God's Word always invites a response. Think about the way the theme of God knowing and speaking to humanity speaks to us today. How does it invite us to respond?

It invites us to prayerfully listen for God's voice and self-revelation in our own life experiences.

It also prompts us to be transparent before God with the awareness that he knows us

completely and still reaches out to us in love.

_____

_____

_____

_____

What is your evaluation of yourself based on any or all of the verses found in John 1?

_____

_____

_____

_____

_____

_____

_____

_____

_____

_____

Our God is a God who speaks.

JOHN 2:23—3:36

In John 3, we find Jesus's conversation with Nicodemus, an encounter that follows John's description in chapter 2 of the inaugural sign of Jesus's ministry: the transformation of water into wine at the wedding in Cana. The water-to-wine miracle is much more than a spectacular sign of Jesus's power—it signals that new life is coming in him. The nature of this new life becomes the focal point of the dialogue between Jesus and Nicodemus.

The critical focus for this section of John's Gospel is the clear articulation of the good news in what is perhaps the most well-known of Bible verses, John 3:16. It is also important to hear this good news in the particular context of Jesus's loving and direct dialogue with Nicodemus—not only in terms of Nicodemus's personal response but also as one who represents the covenant people of God. We can all stand in the place of Nicodemus and hear Jesus speaking these words to us.

WEEK 2, DAY 1

Listen to the story in John 2:23 – 3:36 by reading it aloud several times until you become familiar with its verses, words, and phrases. Enjoy the experience of imagining the story in your mind, picturing each event as it unfolds.

WEEK 2, DAY 2

JOHN 2:23-3:36

The Setting

The context of the meeting with Nicodemus, a Jewish religious official, must have in view the episode in 2:12–22 when Jesus confronts the religious establishment, starting with the commercial interests that have been allowed to take root in and around the Jerusalem temple. Jesus's actions spark a confrontation with the Jews (the religious officials), who demand that Jesus verify his identity through a miraculous sign. To this, Jesus offers the sign of the destruction of the temple, which he says he will raise up in three days. The Jews are incredulous, of course, knowing that it has taken them more than four decades to build the temple, but John explains that Jesus is talking about his body (2:21).

The Synoptic Gospels place this story toward the end of their narratives and connect it to the Passion of Jesus. John's early placement reminds us of how John is approaching his narrative: as a theologically ordered revelation of the identity and nature of Jesus as the Son of God. John uses this story to indicate that God is doing something new in Jesus that will relocate the presence of God on earth from an institution to the life of the Son. This prepares the way for the conversation with Nicodemus, where Jesus's "new wine" message narrows from the religious community to an individual.

The Plot

To discover the plot of John 2:23–3:36, let's divide the passage into eight sections. **Below, summarize or paraphrase the general message or theme of each grouping of verses (following the pattern provided for 2:23–25, 3:1–2, and 3:27–36).**

1. John 2:23–25

When they see the miracles Jesus performs in Jerusalem at the Passover celebration, many people believe in him. But because Jesus knows what is in their hearts, he does not trust them.

2. John 3:1–3

One night a Pharisee named Nicodemus approaches Jesus and declares that Jesus's miracles
prove that he is sent by God. Jesus replies that in order to know God, one must be born again.

3. John 3:4–10

4. John 3:11–15

5. John 3:16–18

6. John 3:19–21

_____

_____

_____

_____

_____

_____

_____

7. John 3:22–26

_____

_____

_____

_____

_____

_____

_____

8. John 3:27–36

John testifies that he is not the Messiah but has been sent to prepare the way for and glorify the Messiah. He testifies that the one sent from heaven speaks on God's behalf and that those who believe in him will be saved.

_____

_____

WORD STUDY NOTES #1

[1] When John says that Jesus "would not entrust himself to them," he is not suggesting Jesus was suspicious or cynical. Rather, it seems that Jesus knows that a faith built solely on signs is insufficient.

WORD STUDY NOTES #2

[1] Jesus begins his response with the Greek words "Amen, amen lego," which is usually translated "I tell you the truth." You will recognize the word "amen." Based on our usage, we may think it means, "I agree with this," but the real emphasis of this construction is more like, "It is true," or, "So be it." It is more than assent; it is a holistic engagement with the truth being proclaimed.

[2] In the Greek, Jesus uses the word anothen, which is translated "from above" or "again." We need to keep both meanings in mind for a correct reading of John 3. Jesus calls us to be "born again" or "born anew," which can only happen as we are "born from above."

[3] The phrase "kingdom of God" is very important in the Synoptic Gospels, and John also includes it in this key story. It has in mind the whole project of what God is doing in Christ Jesus by the power of the Holy Spirit to reconcile all things to God and redeem God's good creation, including us.

What's Happening in the Story?

As we notice certain circumstances in the story, we will begin to see how they are similar to or different from the realities of our world. The story will become the lens through which we see the world in which we live today. In our study today, you may encounter words and/or phrases that are unfamiliar to you. Some of the particular words and translation choices for them have been explained in more detail in the **Word Study Notes**. If you are interested in even more help or detail, you can supplement this study with a Bible dictionary or other Bible study resource.

Practice the pattern you learned in Week 1 to summarize the world and reality that are portrayed in John 2:23–25.

1. John 2:23–25[1]

_____

_____

_____

_____

2. John 3:1–3

Nicodemus does not come to Jesus with questions but with declarations. He comes in the mode of a teacher, even while he acknowledges the role of Jesus as teacher by calling him Rabbi. Nicodemus then goes further by acknowledging that Jesus has come from God. He speaks to Jesus in something of a detached, rather than personal, way. His affirmation seems to include the opinions of his community and clearly reflects the sign-based faith that was the subject of the preceding verses. In response, Jesus turns the moment into a conversation that seems far different from what Nicodemus anticipated. He does this not with argument or direct criticism but with declarative teaching.[1] Jesus flips the motivation for faith from seeing supernatural signs to gaining a new, heavenly birth that allows us to see God's kingdom.[2,3]

3. John 3:4-10

Understandably, Nicodemus asks Jesus how an old person can be born again. The problem is that Nicodemus has no imaginative capacity for Jesus's words beyond the literal and physical. Obviously, he is correct in a literal sense, but what he does not yet see is that Jesus is referring to something qualitatively different than physical birth—it is life from above that makes participation in the reign of God possible here and now.[1] Jesus goes further to help Nicodemus look beyond the obvious, making it clear that he is not speaking of a work according to the flesh but by the Spirit. Nicodemus's incredulity continues as he reiterates his amazement at these ideas. Jesus turns Nicodemus's confidence in verse 2 back on him as he calls into question his position as a teacher of Israel. Then Jesus shifts into lecture mode and begins to lay out for Nicodemus (and for all of us) how this new life from above can become a reality in our lives.

Practice the above pattern to summarize the world and reality that are portrayed in John 3:11-15, 16-18, and 19-21.

4. John 3:11-15[1, 2]

_____

_____

_____

_____

_____

_____

5. John 3:16-18

_____

_____

_____

_____

_____

_____

_____

WORD STUDY NOTES #3

[1] The language "born of water and the Spirit" is an indicator for how Nicodemus should interpret the meaning of "born again." This language indicates that true life is predicated upon birth through a woman (water), which brings bios, physical life. But Jesus is offering zoe, life from above, or life in the Spirit.

WORD STUDY NOTES #4

[1] The image of verse 14, drawn from the story in Numbers 21 of Israel's suffering and healing, offers John's first allusion to the cross and points toward the manner of the Son's exaltation.

[2] The word Jesus uses in verse 14 for "lifted up" (hupsoo) can also mean "exalt." The lifting up of Jesus on a cross, which could be seen as humiliation and defeat, becomes exaltation, victory, and eternal life.

6. John 3:19–21

_____

_____

_____

_____

_____

_____

_____

WORD STUDY NOTES #7

[1] Some manuscripts say "the Jews," which would be consistent with other instances in this Gospel, but either way, we are left without much information about who is bringing this complaint.

7. John 3:22–26

John the Baptist continues baptizing in the Judean countryside, and John's disciples get into an argument with an unnamed Jew about ceremonial washing.[1] John and Jesus are doing ministry at the same time in the same general area, and it is clear that some angst is forming between the two movements. John's disciples come to him and complain about how many people are going to Jesus. While there may be some competitive feelings among the followers, John is very clear about his role. He testifies that he is not the Christ—rather, he has been pointing to the Christ. John uses a parable of a best man and a bridegroom to help his followers remember this.

Create your own brief description of the world and reality portrayed in verses 27–36.

WORD STUDY NOTES #8

[1] Some scholars interpret these words as a later reflection from the author, while others take them as the final testimony of John the Baptist. Either way, these words are consistent with the witness of John the Baptist—the one "from above" is the Son of God in whom there is eternal life.

8. John 3:27–36[1]

_____

_____

_____

_____

_____

_____

_____

Discoveries

Let's summarize our discoveries from John 2:23–3:36.

1. Jesus knows the human heart, and he knows that a faith based on signs and wonders is insufficient and hollow.

2. Jesus taught Nicodemus that a person's experience of salvation at a particular time must be wholly initiated and accomplished by grace in the kingdom of God ("born from above").

3. Jesus is inviting Nicodemus to recognize the element of mystery in spiritual life. Just as the origin of wind was somewhat mysterious to people in the ancient world, so the work of the Spirit has an element of mystery that inspires awe and humility.

4. Jesus is offering a life that is much more than physical thriving (bios); he is offering a quality of life that is "from above" (zoe) and nurtured in God.

5. As Jesus began his ministry, John did not become territorial about followers or claim glory for himself—instead, he sought to diminish himself in order to magnify Jesus as the Messiah.

6. Salvation and hope for eternal life is entirely centered on faith in Jesus as the Son of God who alone gives us eternal life.

If you have a study Bible, it may have references in a margin, a middle column, or footnotes that point to other biblical texts. You may find it helpful in understanding how the whole story of God ties together to look up some of those other scriptures from time to time.

Nicodemus, John the Baptist, and the Story of God

Whenever we read a biblical text, it is important to ask how it relates to the rest of the Bible. **In the space given below, write a short summary of how the themes of genuine faith and God's glory appear in each passage.**

1. Genesis 15:6

_____

_____

_____

_____

_____

_____

2. 1 Samuel 3:1–10

_____

_____

_____

_____

_____

_____

3. 1 Kings 18:36–38

_____

_____

_____

_____

_____

_____

_____

4. Matthew 15:21–28

_____
_____
_____
_____
_____
_____
_____
_____

5. Mark 12:28–34

_____
_____
_____
_____
_____
_____
_____
_____
_____

6. Acts 8:34–38

_____
_____
_____
_____
_____
_____
_____
_____

WEEK 2, DAY 5

John and Our World Today

When we enter into the intriguing narrative of John 2:23—3:36, the story becomes the lens through which we see ourselves, our world, and God's action in our world today.

1. Why is it wrong to base our faith on signs or miracles?

Faith that depends on compelling supernatural evidence is not really faith at all. Demands for signs are rooted in an attitude of selfishness. To require spectacular proofs is to position ourselves as judge and jury over God.

Following the above example, answer these questions about how we understand ourselves, our world, and God's action in our world today.

2. What might we learn from Jesus about how to help people who must take risks or overcome barriers in order to follow him?

3. Following Jesus's lead, how would you explain to an unbeliever what it means to be "born again"?

4. What in your life do you tend to keep in the shadows—something that God might want you to bring into the light?

_____

_____

_____

_____

_____

_____

_____

_____

_____

_____

_____

_____

5. In what ways do we see a spirit of comparison or competition in the life of the church? How do you think the Lord might call us to address these human tendencies?

_____

_____

_____

_____

_____

_____

_____

_____

_____

_____

_____

_____

Invitation and Response

God's Word always invites a response. Think about the way these themes of genuine faith and God's glory speak to us today. How do they invite us to respond?

The text invites us to take Jesus's words to heart and examine our own motivations for belief, asking ourselves to what degree our faith rests on certain signs of God's presence and activity in our lives. It further prompts us to repent of any selfish motivations and testify to the new life in the Spirit that Jesus offers us.

What is your evaluation of yourself based on any or all of the verses found in John 2:23-3:36?

> *A person's experience of salvation must be wholly initiated and accomplished by grace in the kingdom of God.*

JOHN 6

John 6 features the only miracle story that is common to each of the four Gospels: the miraculous feeding of the multitude. In John's narrative, this story follows at some distance from the familiar story of Jesus's encounter with the Samaritan woman at the well and two miraculous healing stories in chapters 4 and 5.

Jesus's encounter with the Samaritan woman is important in establishing Jesus's inclusive, welcoming posture toward the marginalized and outcasts. It is also important in that we see water (something basic and necessary) used as an image of the new life that Jesus brings, as in chapter 2. Jesus helps the woman at the well face the truth about her broken life. He does not condemn her but rather invites her into the refreshment of living water.

Chapters 4 and 5 focus on two healing stories: the royal official's son in Cana and a long-afflicted lame man in Jerusalem. These healing stories lead into a section of Jesus answering the Jews' criticisms.

Chapter 6 begins a new section in the Gospel (6:1–10:42) that mirrors some of the key themes of the first section (2:1–5:47). Where the first section begins with the miracle of wine from water (2:1–11), this second section begins with a miracle of bread.

WEEK 3, DAY 1

Listen to the story in John 6 by reading it aloud several times until you become familiar with its verses, words, and phrases. Enjoy the experience of imagining the story in your mind, picturing each event as it unfolds.

WEEK 3, DAY 2

JOHN 6

The Setting

Chapter 6 features two successive miracles (multiplied bread in verses 1–15 and walking on water in verses 16–21) followed by some dialogue with the crowd, with "the Jews," and with the disciples. The story of the feeding of the multitude in particular clearly occupied a central place in the imagination of the early church and in the way they began to tell the story of Jesus. In fact, Matthew and Mark both seem to tell the story twice (see Matthew 14 and 15; Mark 6 and 8), and there are differences in the tellings that may suggest these are separate incidents. Either way, it is clear that early Christians understood this miracle as a central image of new life in Christ's reign. It is likely that the first Christians connected these stories strongly to their core and regular practice of sharing the Eucharist in worship.

The Plot

To discover the plot of John 6, let's divide the passage into eight sections. **Below, summarize or paraphrase the general message or theme of each grouping of verses (following the pattern provided for verses 1–9, 10–15, and 66–71).**

1. John 6:1–9

After seeing Jesus perform miracles, a crowd of people follows him and his disciples to a

mountainside. Jesus asks his disciple Philip how they will feed the crowd, and Philip is

confounded. Andrew points out that there is a boy among them who has a small portion of

bread and fish, but he cannot see how it could be enough.

2. John 6:10–15

Jesus has the crowd sit down. He takes the bread, blesses it, and serves everyone. He does the same with the fish, and everyone eats their fill. Afterward, he has the disciples gather the uneaten food, and they see that there are still twelve baskets' worth of bread left over. Upon seeing this, the crowd begins to believe that Jesus is a prophet sent by God. Jesus, knowing that they intend to forcibly crown him as their king, secludes himself.

3. John 6:16–24

4. John 6:25–34

5. John 6:35–42

6. John 6:43–58

_____
_____
_____
_____
_____
_____
_____
_____

7. John 6:59–65

_____
_____
_____
_____
_____
_____
_____

8. John 6:66–71

Some of Jesus's disciples stop following him, and Jesus asks the Twelve whether they want to do the same. Peter responds by professing faith that Jesus is sent by God. Jesus notes that although he has chosen them as his followers, one of them will soon betray him.

_____
_____
_____
_____
_____
_____
_____

WEEK 3, DAY 3

What's Happening in the Story?

As we notice certain circumstances in the story, we will begin to see how they are similar to or different from the realities of our world. The story will become the lens through which we see the world in which we live today. In our study today, you may encounter words and/or phrases that are unfamiliar to you. Some of the particular words and translation choices for them have been explained in more detail in the Word Study Notes. If you are interested in even more help or detail, you can supplement this study with a Bible dictionary or other Bible study resource.

1. John 6:1-4

John introduces this story by fixing the location and letting us know that some time has passed between the visit to Jerusalem in chapter 5 and this episode on the lake's far shore. John also references the press of a crowd that gathers in response to Jesus's miracles of healing. Jesus and his disciples now gather on a mountain, which tells us they have moved away from the water's edge, perhaps northeast toward Bethsaida. John also notes that this was near Passover.[1]

2. John 6:5-9

Jesus anticipates the hunger of the gathering crowd and asks Philip where they can get enough bread for them. John lets us know right away that this question was a test—Jesus already knows how he will meet their needs, as well as teach a lesson. Philip does the math and recognizes the sheer impossibility of Jesus's suggestion that they purchase enough bread for the crowd. Then Andrew, in what could be understood either as a ridiculous suggestion or an amazing act of faith, points to a boy who brought a few barley loaves and a couple of dried fish. This little lunch is nearly comical in the face of such a great need, but it forms the basis for the critical point of this story, which Jesus will fully draw out later in the chapter.

WORD STUDY NOTES #1

[1]The mention of Passover is likely more than a note of the calendar; it may also be a reminder of the Exodus story in which bread also features prominently.

49

WORD STUDY NOTES #3

[1] Jesus's actions here are somewhat liturgical, but John seems to liken them more to the normal behavior of a host at a Jewish meal who would take food, give thanks for it, and distribute it to the guests.

[2] In John, Jesus is the one who distributes the multiplied food, whereas in the Synoptics, the disciples do it. John likely means something particular by this detail—that the miracle took place in the Lord's hands, the one who himself is the Bread of life.

[3] Jesus's instruction to gather the leftovers signals not only the scope of the miracle but also a connection with the Exodus manna story, which also features gathering without hoarding (Exodus 16:19).

WORD STUDY NOTES #4

[1] This story about Jesus walking on the water also follows the feeding of the crowds in both Matthew and Mark, which indicates that there was some intentionality in the way these stories were tied together in the early church. The key to these narratives, especially for John, is not the tangible components of the miracles (bread, walking on water), but rather what they reveal about the divine glory revealed in Jesus.

[2] Some translations, such as the NIV, render Jesus's response, "It is I." However, in the context of the whole Gospel, it is clear that Jesus's words are meant to invoke the divine name I Am, as in Exodus 3:14, when God says to Moses, "I am who I am."

[3] Throughout the Bible, when the glory of God is revealed, the common reaction is fear. Yet this is nearly always followed by the reassuring words "do not fear"—the most repeated command in the Bible.

3. John 6:10–15

Jesus instructs the disciples to organize the people by having them sit down on the grass. He then takes the food, blesses it, and distributes it to the crowd.[1,2] The provision is so abundant that Jesus tells the disciples to gather up the food that is left after everyone has had their fill.[3]

Practice the above pattern to summarize the world and reality that are portrayed in verses 16–24.

4. John 6:16–24[1,2,3]

_____

_____

_____

_____

_____

_____

_____

_____

_____

_____

5. John 6:25–27

The crowd's initial question to Jesus about when he arrived seems simple and innocent. Yet Jesus seems to discern something in the motivation behind this question that he begins to confront. In essence, he says they are only following him because of what they think he can do for them—namely, fill their stomachs. Jesus challenges them to pursue not perishable food but eternal, spiritual food, setting up the central theme for the rest of the chapter: what it means for Jesus to be the bread of life.

6. John 6:28–31

The crowd's next question reveals their inability to understand the work Jesus is talking about as anything other than their own effort. So Jesus frames work within a completely different realm than the one they know. But the people persist in their failure to understand Jesus's point, shifting from the question of what *they* must do, to the question of what he will do to prove himself to them. Then they immediately go back to focusing on bread. That's obviously what this boils down to for them—their basic needs.

7. John 6:32–34

Jesus tries again to help them understand bread in a different way. He introduces two key phrases to describe the bread he is talking about: "true bread from heaven" that "gives life to the world." The crowd, still operating on a merely human and natural level, asks him for this bread.[1]

8. John 6:35–42

This passage brings us to the central declaration of chapter six: Jesus calls himself "the bread of life."[1] With this profound declaration, Jesus launches into the first discourse on his identity in which he revisits the gospel preached to Nicodemus in chapter 3. Jesus connects his work to the love and purpose of the Father who has sent him into the world. His only purpose, he says, is to do his Father's will, and everyone who looks to him will enjoy eternal life.

Create your own brief description of the world and reality portrayed in verses 43–58 and 59–65.

_____

_____

_____

_____

_____

WORD STUDY NOTES #7

[1] The crowd's response should remind us of the Samaritan woman's response in John 4:15: "Sir, give me this water." While the crowd and the Samaritan woman recognize that Jesus's offer of bread and water is much better than what their ancestors knew, they still don't comprehend the deeper meaning of Jesus's words.

WORD STUDY NOTES #8

[1] This "I am" statement connects to the other "I am" sayings throughout this Gospel, all of which serve to remind us that Jesus is the Word; Jesus is God.

9. John 6:43-58

_____

_____

_____

_____

_____

_____

WORD STUDY NOTES #10

[1] Jesus's words to the disciples in verses 61–65 remind us that the life Jesus offers is much more than bios (physical life)— it is *zoe* (life from above or life in the Spirit). This distinction is not meant to separate the spiritual from the physical— rather, it is to integrate all of life (heart, mind, soul, and strength) into a holistic response to the grace of God.

10. John 6:59-65[1]

_____

_____

_____

_____

_____

_____

52

WORD STUDY NOTES #11

[1] Peter's language here suggests a kind of certainty and faith. His words indicate that what was formerly enthusiasm and hope has become considered conviction—heart and mind coming together to form a confession of faith.

[2] There is a tension here between divine grace and human will. Jesus clearly acknowledges the place of human will yet is also clear that even our capacity for choosing is a function of grace ("unless the Father has enabled").

11. John 6:66-71

Verse 66 begins with a sobering and somewhat frightening note. How quickly the excitement of the crowd—who were ready to crown Jesus as their king!—turns to disappointment and desertion when they figure out that his kingdom is not of this world. Jesus presses the choice into his group of twelve by asking if they too want to leave. Though Simon Peter jumps in with a declaration of faith,[1] Jesus emphasizes that each of them has the ability to choose faith or doubt, loyalty or betrayal. He notes that he is already aware that one of them has moved toward betrayal.[2] John fills in the details for us, lest we have any doubt that he is talking about Judas Iscariot.

Discoveries

Let's summarize our discoveries from John 6.

1. Jesus anticipated the crowd's needs and took steps to provide for them before they asked. We can draw encouragement from this that the Lord knows and cares about our daily needs.

2. Though the disciples doubted that the small amount of bread and fish would make any difference, Jesus used the small meal to provide more than enough food for the crowd. The key was the transfer of the meager resource from the hands of the boy to the hands of Jesus.

3. Jesus knew that the crowd only sought him out because they wanted him to meet their human needs as he had with the bread and fish. They sought to secure their own lives by trying to put God's provision under their own control.

4. Jesus revealed that he is the bread of life, and that those who believe in him will never be hungry or thirsty again. He is not speaking of mere physical hunger and thirst but of the deepest longings of the heart to know God and be known by God.

5. When they realized that his was not an earthly kingdom, many followers abandoned Jesus. Some were offended that Jesus identified himself with the sustaining bread of heaven. One of Jesus's penetrating questions is offered here: "Do you want to leave too?"

The Bread of Life and the Story of God

Whenever we read a biblical text, it is important to ask how it relates to the rest of the Bible. **In the space given below, write a short summary of how the theme of God's provision for our spiritual nourishment is evident in each passage.**

1. Exodus 16:4–5

_____
_____
_____
_____
_____
_____
_____
_____
_____

2. Psalm 34:10

_____
_____
_____
_____
_____
_____
_____
_____
_____
_____
_____
_____

If you have a study Bible, it may have references in a margin, a middle column, or footnotes that point to other biblical texts. You may find it helpful in understanding how the whole story of God ties together to look up some of those other scriptures from time to time.

54

3. Matthew 6:25–27

_____

_____

_____

_____

_____

_____

4. 2 Corinthians 9:8

_____

_____

_____

_____

_____

_____

5. Philippians 4:18–19

_____

_____

_____

_____

_____

_____

6. 2 Peter 1:3

_____

_____

_____

_____

_____

_____

WEEK 3, DAY 5

John and Our World Today

When we enter into the intriguing narrative of John 6, the story becomes the lens through which we see ourselves, our world, and God's action in our world today.

1. What does the feeding of the multitude tell us about the ways the Lord knows and cares for our needs?

Before we are even aware of our needs, Jesus anticipates and actively addresses them. Even when we can't see a way forward, he knows the best means by which to provide for us.

Following the above example, answer these questions about how we understand ourselves, our world, and God's action in our world today.

2. Verse 6 says that Jesus's question to Philip about feeding the crowd was a test. Do you think the Lord still tests us in these kinds of ways? If so, what might be the purpose of these tests?

3. While the crowd was focused on what Jesus could do for them, Jesus identified himself as "I am," the Lord over all. What might this text teach us about appreciating who God is, and not just what God does?

4. After feeding the crowd, Jesus tells them they must "eat the flesh of the Son of Man and drink his blood," which evokes the church's practice of Communion. What might Jesus's words call us to in our relationship with the body of Christ?

_____

_____

_____

_____

_____

_____

_____

_____

_____

_____

_____

5. While Peter responded to Jesus's question about leaving with a declaration of faith, many of us know people who have turned back from following Jesus. In your own words, how would you respond to Jesus's question in verse 67?

_____

_____

_____

_____

_____

_____

_____

_____

_____

_____

_____

Invitation and Response

God's Word always invites a response. Think about the way the stories of the feeding of the multitude and the bread of life speak to us today. How do they invite us to respond?

We can rest in the assurance that Christ provides us with everything we need—including the times when the way he works doesn't make sense to us. With the assurance that Jesus himself is our sustenance, we can move beyond a preoccupation with our physical desires to prioritize the spiritual food he offers us.

What is your evaluation of yourself based on any or all of the verses found in John 6?

Jesus demonstrates
an inclusive,
welcoming
posture toward
the marginalized
and outcasts.

JOHN 8:12-59

Your Bible may include a note at the end of chapter 7 that reads something like: "The earliest manuscripts and many other ancient witnesses do not have John 7:53–8:11" (NIV). What exactly does this mean? The answer could become a complex discussion, but in the simplest terms, the oldest copies of the New Testament that we have do not include this text in the Gospel of John. Does that mean the story is not true? No; the question is more about the process of gathering these texts into books rather than whether the episode is historical. Clearly, the church found great worth in this beautiful story and, under the direction of the Spirit, began to include it at least as early as the fourth century. We continue to find great worth in the story because it is consistent in every way with what the Gospels reveal to us about Jesus.

Nevertheless, we begin our study this week with verse 12 to emphasize the theological theme of this chapter. Jesus begins with another "I am" statement, which connects us immediately with similar instances throughout this Gospel. Whereas in chapter 6 Jesus said, "I am the bread of life," here Jesus says, "I am the light of the world." This confession sets up the rest of the chapter in which we will see in the debates between Jesus and "the Jews" (John's shorthand for the religious leaders) the difference between walking in light and walking in darkness. Again, we are taken back to where John's narrative began as he declared, "The light shines in the darkness, and the darkness has not overcome it" (1:5).

60

WEEK 4, DAY 1

Listen to the story in John 8:12–59 by reading it aloud several times until you become familiar with its verses, words, and phrases. Enjoy the experience of imagining the story in your mind, picturing each event as it unfolds.

WEEK 4, DAY 2

JOHN 8:12-59

The Setting

This chapter comes to us in the context of Jesus going to the Feast of Tabernacles in chapter 7. The lighting of lamps was a key feature of the celebration during the Feast of Tabernacles, with the lighting of four large lampstands in the Temple Court of Women marking the end of the first day. The light from these lamps could be seen throughout the city. Celebrants danced in the courtyard with their own torches, adding even more light to the nighttime festival, all in joyful remembrance of God's deliverance of the people from slavery and pointing to their renewed hope that God might once again deliver them from oppression. This is the setting of verse 12, where we hear Jesus proclaim, "I am the light of the world."

As we walk through chapter 8, verse 12 needs to be kept at the top of every page as a guiding light from which the unfolding story is interpreted. Jesus's self-identification as the light of the world confirms what John said about him in the beginning of this Gospel. John claims from the beginning that the Word is light and life and that the purpose of this light is not simply to display God's own glory but also to provide light for the whole world by which every person can believe and become children of God (1:12). On this basis, Jesus himself now essentially repeats John's testimony from chapter 1 and invites all who will to follow him so that we might "never walk in darkness, but . . . have the light of life" (8:12).

The Plot

To discover the plot of John 8:12–59, let's divide the passage into six sections. **Below, summarize or paraphrase the general message or theme of each grouping of verses (following the pattern provided for verses 12–13, 14–18, and 48–59).**

1. John 8:12–13

Jesus proclaims to a gathered crowd that he is the light of the world and that those who follow him will have life. The Pharisees scoff at his self-proclamation.

2. John 8:14–18

Jesus replies that his testimony is true because he and the Father stand together, and the Father is his witness. While the Pharisees judge by human standards, Jesus judges according to the Father's standards.

3. John 8:19–30

4. John 8:31–32

5. John 8:33–47

6. John 8:48–59

Jesus answers the Jews' accusations against him. He says he seeks to honor his Father and that those who obey him will not die. The Jews say he is possessed if he claims to be greater than Abraham and the prophets of Israel who died. Jesus says any glory he has comes from the Father and that Abraham rejoiced in seeing his ministry. The Jews say that it is impossible for him to have met Abraham. Jesus invokes the words of God's self-revelation, declaring that he existed before Abraham was born. The Jews are ready to stone Jesus for this, but he escapes before they can kill him.

WEEK 4, DAY 3

What's Happening in the Story?

As we notice certain circumstances in the story, we will begin to see how they are similar to or different from the realities of our world. The story will become the lens through which we see the world in which we live today. In our study today, you may encounter words and/or phrases that are unfamiliar to you. Some of the particular words and translation choices for them have been explained in more detail in the **Word Study Notes**. If you are interested in even more help or detail, you can supplement this study with a Bible dictionary or other Bible study resource.

1. John 8:12–13

Verse 12 begins with Jesus speaking to a Jerusalem crowd that would have included Jewish families who had come for the festival. To this crowd, Jesus identifies himself as the light of the world and proclaims that those who follow him will no longer have to walk in darkness. Immediately, the Pharisees attempt to dismiss Jesus's claims. Their approach is to discredit his words on the basis of insufficient witnesses.[1]

2. John 8:14–18

Jesus says that his testimony is valid because he and the Father stand together.[1] The real issue is what Jesus states in verse 15: the Pharisees judge by human standards.[2] The Pharisees are willing to see only what is obvious, but Jesus is pointing them to that which is divine and eternal. We see an important distinction between how Jesus judges and how Pharisees judge. While the Pharisees judge from pride and fear, which leads to condemnation, Jesus's judgment is to bring life.

_____

_____

_____

_____

WORD STUDY NOTES #1

[1] Jewish law required that, in order for a testimony to be considered valid, it must be accompanied by two witnesses. Jesus brings up this requirement himself in 5:31-40 when he names two witnesses on his behalf: John the Baptist and the Father.

WORD STUDY NOTES #2

[1] Unlike the episode in chapter 5, in which Jesus argues on the basis of law, here Jesus shifts from the framework of human law to the larger question of his identity as the Word who makes the Father known.

[2] The Greek words here are _kata tén sarka_, which literally translates, "according to the flesh." Jesus's charge that the Pharisees judge by human standards refers to their unwillingness to see and their unbelief in what God is doing.

WORD STUDY NOTES #3

[1] Jesus will later describe this place as "my Father's house" (14:2).

3. John 8:19–30

Jesus keeps working to show his interlocutors that he is not simply the son of a father in the manner to which they are accustomed. He speaks of departing to a place above.[1] All the Pharisees can think is that he plans to kill himself, which prompts Jesus to point out again that they are only thinking in earth-bound and human terms. He is speaking of life "from above," which can only be rightly discerned by faith, and he tells them that, unless they believe, they will die in their sins. When they are still unable to see, Jesus finally gets to the bottom line: only when they have lifted him up (a clear reference to the cross) will they know. In the very act of seeking to do away with Jesus, they will exalt him to a place from which they will be confronted with the truth of his claims in new and powerful ways.

WORD STUDY NOTES #4

[1] Some scholars think that the Pharisees are interpreting Jesus's words more spiritually than historically. That is, as children of Abraham, they are already free in that they have been chosen by God, and thus have no need of what Jesus is offering.

[2] When Jesus speaks about truth, he is not talking so much about a body of knowledge (although knowledge is included) as he is about a humble posture of responsiveness—of following him so closely that our lives begin to look, sound, and feel like his.

[3] Ironically, the Pharisees forget not only that they *have* known slavery in their history but also that even now, they chafe under the yoke of Rome's oppression.

4. John 8:31–33

In these verses we find a sustained theological debate between Jesus and the Jewish leaders. While the Jews are focused on their relationship to Abraham, Jesus wants to focus their attention on their relationship with God.[1] Jesus's declaration that "the truth will set you free" is key to this section.[2] Jesus makes clear what is required for living in truth: to hold to his teaching. There are important conditions for the capacity to live in the freedom of truth. Unfortunately, the Pharisees are so focused on themselves and their traditions that they cannot really hear what Jesus is saying. They immediately take offense at the suggestion that they need freedom, imagining themselves already to be free as the chosen people of God—they claim they have never been slaves.[3] This launches a long debate that occupies the rest of the chapter.

Practice the above pattern to summarize the world and reality that are portrayed in verses 34–38, 39–41, 42–47, 48–51, and 52–59 .

_____

_____

_____

_____

5. John 8:34–38

_____

_____

_____

_____

_____

_____

_____

_____

6. John 8:39–41

_____

_____

_____

_____

_____

_____

_____

_____

7. John 8:42–47

_____

_____

_____

_____

_____

_____

_____

_____

_____

[1] Jesus's language in verse 49 evokes the well-accepted notion of honor in the ancient Near Eastern world—that the one sent is the same as the sender. Jesus also works with this idea of honor in chapter 5 when he responds to the Pharisees' criticism for healing on the Sabbath.

8. John 8:48–51[1]

_____

_____

_____

_____

_____

_____

_____

_____

_____

_____

_____

_____

9. John 8:52–59

_____

_____

_____

_____

_____

_____

_____

_____

_____

_____

_____

_____

Discoveries

Let's summarize some of our discoveries from John 8:12–59.

1. Jesus identified himself to a crowd in Jerusalem as the light who breaks through the world's spiritual darkness.

2. Although we make our journey in a sometimes-dark world, Jesus promises us light and life for the journey.

3. Jesus's testimony is valid because he stands with his Father, who is his witness. The Pharisees did not understand this because they judged only by human standards.

4. When Jesus told the Pharisees that he was departing to a place they could not follow, they did not understand him—they were still thinking in narrow human terms. Jesus knew they would only understand once they had crucified him.

5. When Jesus told the Pharisees that the truth of his teachings would set them free, they argued that they were already free because of their connection with Abraham. But Jesus's teaching represented a paradigm shift. He said it was their relationship with God through him, God's own Son, that truly mattered and that if they rejected him, they also rejected God.

6. Truth is not simply knowledge about something. It is intimate relationship with someone (Jesus) who knows everything about us.

7. The Pharisees were generally good people—they were conservative holiness people. The problem was that their conservatism became idolatrous when they imagined their faith could be secured by a tight set of doctrines.

8. The Jews accused Jesus of being an outsider and of being demon-possessed. Jesus replied that he honored his Father, who sent him and entrusted him with his power. He then identified himself by invoking the divine name—"I am." His words sounded blasphemous to his questioners, who were so outraged that they attempted to kill him before he escaped.

The Light of the World and the Story of God

Whenever we read a biblical text, it is important to ask how it relates to the rest of the Bible. **In the space given below, write a short summary of how the themes of light and darkness are discussed in each passage.**

1. Genesis 1:1–3

_____

_____

_____

_____

_____

_____

_____

2. Isaiah 60:1
The prophet uses the metaphor of light to project the ways that God's redemptive work among his people will restore their glory and lead them from their darkness.

_____

_____

_____

3. Acts 26:18

_____

_____

_____

_____

_____

_____

_____

_____

If you have a study Bible, it may have references in a margin, a middle column, or footnotes that point to other biblical texts. You may find it helpful in understanding how the whole story of God ties together to look up some of those other scriptures from time to time.

70

4. Ephesians 5:8

_____
_____
_____
_____
_____
_____
_____
_____
_____

5. 1 Peter 2:9

_____
_____
_____
_____
_____
_____
_____
_____
_____

6. 1 John 2:9–11

_____
_____
_____
_____
_____
_____
_____
_____
_____

WEEK 4, DAY 5

John and Our World Today

When we enter into the intriguing narrative of John 8:12–59, the story becomes the lens through which we see ourselves, our world, and God's action in our world today.

1. What can we take away from the Pharisees' responses to Jesus in this passage?

When reading the Gospels, it could be tempting to quickly critique and dismiss the Pharisees. But it is important to remember that, as their responses reveal, these were generally good people—they were the conservatives, the Holiness people. The problem was that their conservatism became idolatrous; they believed that their faith could be secured by a tight set of doctrines. While their opposition to Jesus is worthy of critique, we should first consider any pharisaical tendencies in ourselves that prevent us from hearing his voice.

Following the above example, answer these questions about how we understand ourselves, our world, and God's action in our world today.

2. In what ways can our view of how God works be limited by narrow, legalistic human standards?

3. Consider Jesus's words about truth in verses 31–47. To what degree are you living in the truth he describes?

_____

_____

_____

_____

_____

_____

_____

4. What tightly held tradition, philosophy, or even theology might be preventing you from hearing Jesus's voice in new ways?

_____

_____

_____

_____

_____

_____

_____

_____

5. Think about the ways that our world seeks to minimize or discredit Jesus's true identity as the Son of God. What can we learn from Jesus's interactions with doubters?

_____

_____

_____

_____

_____

_____

_____

_____

Invitation and Response

God's Word always invites a response. Think about the way these themes of light and darkness speak to us today. How do they invite us to respond?

The text invites us to recognize the sin in the world and in ourselves for what it is—spiritual darkness that can only be dispelled by the light of Jesus. This in turn gives us the opportunity to evaluate and repent of any narrow human standards that may limit our ability to hear Jesus's voice in new and fresh ways.

What is your evaluation of yourself based on any or all of the verses found in John 8:12–59?

We should consider
any pharisaical
tendencies in
ourselves that
prevent us from
hearing God's voice.

JOHN 11

The central story of John 11—the raising of Lazarus from the dead—is not just an amazing and powerful story. It further reveals a key theme of John's Gospel—another "I am" revelation from Jesus. This time, Jesus declares he is the one with divine authority over death itself. This chapter sets up the close of what scholars have called the Book of Signs (chapters 1–12) and begins the transition into the Book of Glory (chapters 13–20). When we get to verse 45, it may seem as though the end of chapter 11 is disconnected from the first 44 verses, but chapters 11 and 12 can be taken as a unit of narration that sets up the journey toward the cross that begins in chapter 13.

In most of John's miracle stories, the miracle is followed by a section of teaching or discourse. Here, the miracle at the end of the chapter will be preceded by the movement and dialogue of the many characters in the story (Lazarus, Mary, Martha, Jesus, the disciples, Thomas, the community). The conversation among these characters is foundational to the theological theme John advances as we move toward the total unfolding of Jesus's identity and mission in the rest of the Gospel.

76

WEEK 5, DAY 1

Listen to the story in John 11 by reading it aloud several times until you become famil-iar with its verses, words, and phrases. Enjoy the experience of imagining the story in your mind, picturing each event as it unfolds.

WEEK 5, DAY 2

JOHN 11

The Setting

The story of the raising of Lazarus is unique to the book of John. For the Synoptic Gospels (Matthew, Mark, and Luke), the story of Jesus cleansing the temple precipitates his suffering and death. For John, the story of Lazarus plays that role. The Synoptics also include a raising-the-dead story, but for them, it is the raising of Jairus's daughter (Matthew 9; Mark 5; Luke 8). The point is that this account, like the Jairus story in the Synoptics, is meant as more than a fascinating story of Jesus's power to perform miracles; it is meant as a sign of Jesus's identity—the identity that John has been preaching all the way along. Here, the sign prepares us to walk with Jesus toward the cross, not in despair but in hope.

The Plot

To discover the plot of John 11, let's divide the passage into six sections. **Below, summarize or paraphrase the general message or theme of each grouping of verses (following the pattern provided for verses 1–5, 6–10, and 45–57).**

1. John 11:1–5

Jesus's friend Lazarus is sick. His sisters send a message to Jesus about their brother's illness. When he hears it, Jesus says that Lazarus will not die and that his sickness will be used for the glory of God and God's son.

2. John 11:6–10

After staying in place for two days and learning that Lazarus has died, Jesus decides to go back to Judea. His disciples object, since people there recently tried to stone Jesus, but Jesus replies that those who walk in the light will not stumble.

3. John 11:11–16

---

4. John 11:17–37

---

5. John 11:38–44

_____

_____

_____

_____

_____

_____

_____

_____

_____

_____

_____

_____

6. John 11:45–57

The people who saw Jesus raise Lazarus from the dead believe in him, but when the Pharisees hear about it, they plot to kill Jesus in order to keep the peace. Jesus retreats to a remote area with his disciples. People look for Jesus in Jerusalem as the Passover festival approaches, but the religious officials have a warrant out for his arrest.

_____

_____

_____

_____

_____

_____

_____

_____

_____

_____

WEEK 5, DAY 3

What's Happening in the Story?

As we notice certain circumstances in the story, we will begin to
see how they are similar to or different from the realities of our
world. The story will become the lens through which we see the
world in which we live today. In our study today, you may encounter words and/or phrases that are unfamiliar to you. Some of
the particular words and translation choices for them have been
explained in more detail in the **Word Study Notes**. If you are
interested in even more help or detail, you can supplement this
study with a Bible dictionary or other Bible study resource.

1. John 11:1–5

The beginning of this passage sets up the context in which this
miracle will unfold. We learn that the main character is Lazarus
from Bethany.[1] Lazarus is the brother of Mary and Martha, who
are clearly part of Jesus's inner circle during his ministry—
John says that Jesus loves them.[2, 3] The critical point of these
introductory verses comes when Jesus turns the focus away
from the illness and even the possibility of Lazarus's death to
the larger question of how God's glory will be revealed through
this difficult episode.[4]

_____

_____

_____

_____

_____

_____

_____

_____

_____

_____

_____

WORD STUDY NOTES #1

[1] Bethany appears to be
where Jesus stayed when
he visited Jerusalem (see
Mark 11:11; 14:3).

[2] This family was no
doubt well known among
the earliest followers of
Jesus, but John further
establishes the context by
explaining that this Mary
is the one who anointed
Jesus. Interestingly, that
story is not told until John
12, but John inserts the
reference here—no doubt
because it was already
so well known and would
serve to make clear which
family is in view.

[3] The sisters' faith in Jesus
is suggested by their quick
realization that they need
to call for Jesus's aid as
they try to care for their
sick brother.

[4] The irony of Jesus's
words is that, while this
illness is not the ultimate
end for Lazarus's life, it will
lead to Jesus's own death.

2. John 11:6–10

Upon hearing of the desperate situation in Bethany, Jesus inexplicably decides to remain where he is for two more days. If we read John closely, we understand this is not a matter of Jesus being delayed by something else. John makes a point to highlight that Jesus consciously decided to stay in place.[1] Later, Jesus decides to move back toward Judea, which is incredible to the disciples given the threats that Jesus experienced there. Jesus's response to their concerns brings back John's emphasis on the motif of light and darkness—Jesus locates his work in the light, in which there is nothing to fear. Death is not the enemy—walking in darkness is.

3. John 11:11–16

Jesus puts the issue of Lazarus's death into a perspective that will change the disciples' understanding of death, resurrection, and the power of God. Jesus knows what has not yet been reported—that Lazarus has died. He says that Lazarus has fallen asleep,[1] which confuses the disciples because why would Jesus go back and face threats if Lazarus is only asleep? Jesus clarifies that Lazarus *has* died, then gives the disciples the real reason for his delay: it is so that they might believe.

Practice the above pattern to summarize the world and reality that are portrayed in verses 17–37, 38–44, and 45–57.

_____

_____

_____

_____

_____

_____

_____

_____

_____

_____

_____

4. John 11:17–37[1,2,3]

_____

_____

_____

_____

_____

_____

_____

_____

_____

_____

_____

_____

_____

_____

_____

_____

_____

_____

_____

_____

_____

_____

_____

_____

_____

_____

_____

_____

_____

WORD STUDY NOTES #4

[1] The Jews believed one should visit a tomb daily for three days to make sure the person was really dead. Rabbis taught that the soul would remain around a grave and try to return to the body but would finally give up if the body did not come back to life after three days.

[2] The words "resurrection" and "life" may seem like synonyms. However, a closer examination reveals that Jesus is speaking not only of life after death (resurrection) but also of a way of living here and now in the light and hope of resurrection (life).

[3] Scholars note that the phrase in verse 33 that is usually translated "deeply moved" (NIV) or "greatly disturbed" (NRSV) reflects a sense of anger or indignation more so than a sense of compassion. Perhaps the most likely interpretation is that Jesus is angry about the brokenness of God's good creation that is marred by the enemy, death.

WORD STUDY NOTES #5

[1] The phrase translated "deeply moved" in verse 38 is the same phrase that appears in verse 33. Once again, John highlights Jesus's anger as well as his compassion. Here, his anger may be connected to the Jews' doubtful and accusatory remarks in verse 37.

[2] Jesus's command to "Take away the stone" in verse 39 foreshadows the greatest miracle of all on Easter morning.

[3] In verse 41, Jesus looks to heaven and prays. While this is Jesus's characteristic way of praying in the Synoptic Gospels—he "lifts up" his countenance and addresses God as his Father—this is the first time in the book of John that Jesus addresses God as "Father."

WORD STUDY NOTES #6

[1] Ironically, in his prophecy, Caiaphas unwittingly proclaims the power of Jesus's death to save the nation and "the scattered children of God" (11:52).

5. John 11:38–44[1, 2, 3]

_____
_____
_____
_____
_____
_____
_____
_____
_____
_____
_____
_____
_____

6. John 11:45–57[1]

_____
_____
_____
_____
_____
_____
_____
_____
_____
_____
_____
_____
_____
_____

Discoveries

Let's summarize some of our discoveries from John 11.

1. When Mary and Martha informed Jesus of Lazarus's illness, Jesus did not rush to his friend's side—instead, he intentionally stayed where he was. Though Jesus grieved when he learned of Lazarus's death, he knew that his waiting would glorify God and bring people to faith.

2. A difficult and life-changing thing happens (Lazarus dies), but Jesus seems to have a perspective about it that keeps him free of fear or anxiety.

3. Mary and Martha were grieved by Jesus's delay because they had faith that Jesus could have healed Lazarus if he had arrived in time. But Jesus declared that he himself is the source of resurrection and life and that those who believe in him will not die.

4. Reflecting on Jesus's human responses in this text, we notice his love for this family, his relationship with the sisters who are deep in grief, his anger at suffering and the condition of the world, his personal sense of loss, and his empathy for the pain of others.

5. While we know that Jesus could have met this need immediately, we see him withdraw and wait for the right time. We may struggle with times of waiting, but Jesus shows us that waiting can bring great blessing.

6. In an act that prefigured his own resurrection, Jesus raised the long-dead Lazarus from the grave, and the witnesses who saw it believed in him.

7. After learning of the miracle and fearing it would threaten their authority, the religious rulers began plotting to kill Jesus. They reasoned that they would be justified in taking one life to save many. They did not know that Jesus was indeed prepared to give his life to save the people—all the people of the world.

The Raising of Lazarus and the Story of God

Whenever we read a biblical text, it is important to ask how it relates to the rest of the Bible. **In the space given below, write a short summary of how the theme of resurrection is discussed in each passage.**

1. 1 Kings 17:17–24

_____

_____

_____

_____

_____

_____

_____

_____

_____

_____

2. Isaiah 26:19

_____

_____

_____

_____

_____

_____

_____

_____

If you have a study Bible, it may have references in a margin, a middle column, or footnotes that point to other biblical texts. You may find it helpful in understanding how the whole story of God ties together to look up some of those other scriptures from time to time.

3. Luke 7:11–15

_____
_____
_____
_____
_____
_____
_____
_____

4. Acts 20:7–12

_____
_____
_____
_____
_____
_____
_____
_____

5. Romans 8:11

_____
_____
_____
_____
_____
_____
_____
_____
_____

6. 1 Corinthians 15:51–54

7. Philippians 3:10–11

WEEK 5, DAY 5

John and Our World Today

When we enter into the intriguing narrative of John 11, the story becomes the lens through which we see ourselves, our world, and God's action in our world today.

1. What does Jesus's delay in visiting Lazarus teach us about how God answers our prayers?

God operates according to God's own timing. Like Mary and Martha, discrepancies between

God's timing and ours may confuse us or even lead us to think God is neglecting our requests.

But this is not the case—God loves us and is always working to respond in ways that draw

people into the resurrection life.

_____

_____

Following the above example, answer these questions about how we understand ourselves, our world, and God's action in our world today.

2. What does Jesus's reaction to Lazarus's death teach us about how we view suffering and death?

_____

_____

_____

_____

_____

_____

_____

_____

_____

_____

_____

_____

3. What difference does the resurrection make in this moment—in your personal situation and/or the state of the world around you?

_____

_____

_____

_____

_____

_____

_____

_____

_____

_____

_____

_____

4. In what ways are we tempted to become so self-assured and controlling in our religious practices that we risk being on the wrong side of God's work altogether?

_____

_____

_____

_____

_____

_____

_____

_____

_____

_____

_____

_____

Invitation and Response

God's Word always invites a response. Think about the way the story of the raising of Lazarus speaks to us today. How does it invite us to respond?

This story invites us to rejoice in the hope of resurrection and give thanks that, just as Jesus raised Lazarus from the dead, he has also raised us from our spiritual death. It also reminds us that, although God's timing does not always correspond to ours, God is always working to heal the damage caused by sin and death, and he himself is our life.

What is your evaluation of yourself based on any or all of the verses found in John 11?

Jesus is never to be understood as
uncaring or undisciplined; his timing is
determined by his mission from the Father.

Week Six: Promise of the Spirit

JOHN 14–17

Chapter 14 begins what scholars have often termed the Book of Glory. While it may seem that the Jews' plot to get rid of Jesus is the driving force behind these chapters, we should remember what Jesus says to Pilate in chapter 19: "You would have no power over me if it were not given to you from above" (v. 11). The focal point of these chapters is on Jesus preparing to lay down his life. Accordingly, chapters 14–17 are often called the Farewell Discourse, although there is considerable difference of opinion regarding the boundaries of the text. Since the narrative setting seems to run from 14:1–17:26, that is the scope we have in view for our study this week. Our task will be to learn the theological movements of the texts against the backdrop of John's overall project in his Gospel.

For organizational and thematic purposes, we will explore four units that offer us the core themes of the discourse:

Chapter 14: "I will not leave you as orphans" (verse 18)

Chapter 15: "Remain in me, as I also remain in you" (verse 4)

Chapter 16: "I will send [the Counselor] to you" (verse 7)

Chapter 17: "The hour has come. Glorify your Son" (verse 1)

WEEK 6, DAY 1

Listen to the story in John 14–17 by reading it aloud several times until you become familiar with its verses, words, and phrases. Enjoy the experience of imagining the story in your mind, picturing each event as it unfolds.

WEEK 6, DAY 2

JOHN 14-17

The Setting

Remember that the chapter and verse markings of the Bible came as later additions to the text, so we should read the beginning of chapter 14 as a continuation of the dialogue that is happening at the end of chapter 13, where we sense the disciples' separation anxiety as Jesus explicitly discusses his imminent departure.

Unlike other discourse sections in John's Gospel, in these chapters, Jesus is not simply responding to the immediate situation. His view has now expanded to the overarching vision of his purpose in the world. He is on his way to the Father, and his loving concern for those he will leave behind comes through. Jesus works to prepare them and to shape a hopeful imagination in them that will recast their understanding of Jesus from their beloved Rabbi to the crucified, resurrected, and ascended Lord Jesus Christ.

The Plot

To discover the plot of John 14–17, let's divide the passage into eight sections. **Below, summarize or paraphrase the general message or theme of each grouping of verses (following the pattern provided for John 14, 15:1–8, and John 16).**

1. John 14

Jesus tells his disciples that he will prepare a place for them in his Father's house. The disciples want to go with him and see the Father, but Jesus says that they have already seen the Father in him. He promises that God will send his Spirit as an advocate for them in his absence.

_____

_____

2. John 15:1–8

Jesus is the true vine, and his Father is the gardener. He tells the disciples that they are the branches-if they remain connected to him, they will bear fruit. Otherwise, they will wither and die.

_____

_____

3. John 15:9–17

4. John 15:18–27

5. John 16

The time is coming when people will persecute the disciples because of their association with Jesus. Jesus is going back to his Father, which grieves the disciples. But Jesus promises that their grief will turn to joy and that they will be connected to the Father through him.

6. John 17:1–5

_____
_____
_____
_____
_____
_____
_____
_____
_____

7. John 17:6–19

_____
_____
_____
_____
_____
_____
_____
_____
_____

8. John 17:20–26

_____
_____
_____
_____
_____
_____
_____
_____

WEEK 6, DAY 3

What's Happening in the Story?

As we notice certain circumstances in the story, we will begin to see how they are similar to or different from the realities of our world. The story will become the lens through which we see the world in which we live today. In our study today, you may encounter words and/or phrases that are unfamiliar to you. Some of the particular words and translation choices for them have been explained in more detail in the **Word Study Notes**. If you are interested in even more help or detail, you can supplement this study with a Bible dictionary or other Bible study resource.

1. John 14

We enter this chapter in the wake of the disciples' separation anxiety as Jesus discusses his imminent departure. Jesus notes their troubled hearts. The whole chapter has in view their continuing mission in the world in service to the gospel. They are being challenged to trust, to stand firm, to believe that Jesus is indeed the Son of God. Jesus sounds the hope of his final victory, in which all who believe are included. When Jesus says he is preparing a place for his disciples, he means that he is headed to the cross. He is going to prepare the new reality that his death and resurrection will make available to those who believe.[1] The disciples have a hard time imagining anything other than spatial reality. Thomas directly challenges Jesus's statement that they know the way, which prompts yet another of Jesus's powerful "I am" expressions in the Gospel of John. This reaffirms that Jesus is not talking about a destination but about a type of life, in which to know the way is to know Jesus.[2] It also reveals Jesus as the Word who was "with God" and "was God" (1:1). This sets up Jesus's response to Philip, in which he strengthens his identification with the Father. The rest of chapter 14 focuses on the promise of the Holy Spirit.[3] The language of these verses makes it evident that the work of the Spirit is the work of Jesus. The Spirit of truth is in complete unity with the Father and the Son. As Jesus's teaching continues in this passage, he tells his disciples that their life in him through the Spirit is not only meant

WORD STUDY NOTES #1

[1] It is easy to read these verses as Jesus speaking of heaven, where we have popularized the notion of heavenly mansions being prepared for the faithful to abide in the final day. In one sense this is true, but when John speaks of "my Father's house," we need to keep in mind that throughout this Gospel, the idea of residence is more relational than locational.

[2] One of the earliest terms that believers and nonbelievers alike used for Jesus's new movement was "the way" (see Acts 9:2).

[3] Here, in describing the Spirit, John's Gospel introduces a new word: paraclete. This word is rich with meaning and speaks of comfort, encouragement, help, consolation, and more. It describes not only who the Spirit is but also the way the Spirit works.

[4] When he promises peace to the disciples, Jesus uses a word (eirene) that speaks less of security or lack of conflict and more about a well-being and wholeness that rise from the life of Jesus in us.

for their security and sense of identity but is also for mission. Jesus is about to live his life through his disciples. As this unfolds, Jesus offers a beautiful assurance of peace to strengthen them.[4]

2. John 15:1–8

This chapter opens with the final "I am" saying in John's Gospel. Jesus identifies himself as the vine that gives life to the branches and thus to the fruit.[1] Jesus is the true vine[2] because he comes from the Father (a theme we have seen throughout John), who is the gardener. As the gardener, the Father brings judgment upon the vine through the necessary work of pruning.[3] Jesus says the key to keeping this vital connection is to remain in him—which happens through remaining in his word.[4]

Practice the above pattern to summarize the world and reality that are portrayed in John 15:9–17, 18–27, and chapter 16.

3. John 15:9–17

_____

_____

_____

_____

_____

_____

4. John 15:18–27

_____

_____

_____

_____

_____

_____

_____

WORD STUDY NOTES #2

[1] The metaphor of Israel as a vineyard is often used in the Old Testament. The prophets use this image to describe God as one who plants and tends.

[2] Jesus's declaration that he is the _true_ vine suggests that there are other vines that offer themselves as a source for life but cannot actually produce it.

[3] The note about pruning implies that the barren branches are not completely outside the economy of God's vineyard when they become unfruitful. The problem is, they are not connected in life-giving ways.

[4] Some translations have "abide" instead of "remain," but the idea in this word is "stay here."

5. John 16

_____

_____

_____

_____

_____

_____

_____

_____

6. John 17:1-5

As Jesus lifts up his head and prays, we remember that this prayer comes at the conclusion of his meal with the disciples (see 13:2), in which all of these profound questions and responses have been spoken. And it has all been happening under the specter of "the hour" that has come. But now Jesus speaks of this hour explicitly and frames it not in terms of inevitability or tragedy but in terms of glory. He prays to the Father for glory in his presence. In this petition, the Gospel's message is emerging through Jesus's unfolding mission to lay down his life.

Create your own brief description of the world and reality portrayed in verses 6–19.

WORD STUDY NOTES #7

[1] In his prayer, Jesus says his disciples will carry the message and mission of the gospel into the world. This tells us that their selection as disciples was no incidental decision but one of purpose and prayer.

7. John 17:6-19[1]

_____

_____

_____

_____

_____

_____

_____

8. John 17:20-26

Jesus's prayer turns to all those who believe in him through the testimony and faithful witness of his first followers. In his prayer, he focuses especially on unity not for its own sake but so that the world might see the unity of the Father, Son, and Spirit reflected in the body of Christ. It is by witnessing this, Jesus says, that the world[1] will realize that God sent him and that God loves them. The unity of Jesus's followers will make the holy love of God (as expressed in the holy fellowship of the Trinity) visible to the world.

_____

_____

_____

_____

_____

_____

_____

_____

_____

_____

WORD STUDY NOTES #8

[1] In this expression, Jesus no longer depicts the world as hating the disciples (as in earlier passages) but as receiving the witness of the disciples in a way that brings them to faith.

101

Discoveries

Let's summarize some of our discoveries from John 14–17.

1. Jesus assured his disciples that he would prepare a place for them in his Father's house and encouraged them to love him by keeping his commands. He promised them that the Father would send the Spirit of truth to be their helper and advocate as they kept the faith after his departure.

2. While we certainly know and celebrate our hope of eternal life, this passage also speaks to us about the kind of life Jesus is inviting us to experience here and now.

3. Jesus taught his disciples that he is the vine, they are the branches, and the Father is the gardener. To remain fruitful, they must remain connected to him, their source.

4. Jesus suggests that the center of what it means to remain in him is to know his love and live in his love. This is not individual or private—it is known in how we love one another.

5. Jesus told the disciples that he would soon leave them, and that people would persecute and kill them for their association with him. He said that while these events would cause them grief, their sorrow would turn to joy because they would have a relationship with the Father through him.

6. Jesus prayed for God to be glorified and to glorify him as he made the way for people to have eternal life. He then prayed for his disciples, committing them to God's protection, and prayed for unity for those who would come to believe in him through the disciples' testimony.

7. Just as Jesus does not "belong" to this world (not speaking of creation but the principalities and powers that are in opposition to the reign of God), neither do his followers belong to the world.

WEEK 6, DAY 4

The Vineyard, the Spirit, and the Story of God

Whenever we read a biblical text, it is important to ask how it relates to the rest of the Bible. **In the space given below, write a short summary of how the theme of God's life-giving power appears in each passage.**

1. Genesis 2:7

_____

_____

_____

_____

_____

_____

2. 1 Chronicles 29:10–13

_____

_____

_____

_____

_____

_____

3. Jeremiah 10:12–13

_____

_____

_____

_____

_____

_____

_____

If you have a study Bible, it may have references in a margin, a middle column, or footnotes that point to other biblical texts. You may find it helpful in understanding how the whole story of God ties together to look up some of those other scriptures from time to time.

4. Ezekiel 37:9–10

_____

_____

_____

_____

_____

_____

5. Matthew 19:26

_____

_____

_____

_____

_____

_____

6. 1 Corinthians 6:14

_____

_____

_____

_____

_____

_____

7. Ephesians 1:19–21

_____

_____

_____

_____

_____

_____

WEEK 6, DAY 5

John and Our World Today

When we enter into the intriguing narrative of John 14–17, the story becomes the lens through which we see ourselves, our world, and God's action in our world today.

1. What does John 14–17 tell us about the kind of life Jesus offers us?

Jesus offers us not only the hope of eternal life after death but also the here-and-now new life

that comes with being born again.

_____

_____

_____

_____

_____

_____

Following the above example, answer these questions about how we understand ourselves, our world, and God's action in our world today.

2. What do you think it means to remain in Christ? What are the practices or disciplines that help you do so?

_____

_____

_____

_____

_____

_____

_____

_____

_____

_____

_____

_____

_____

_____

3. What can we learn from Jesus's prayer about the relationship among the Father, Son, and Spirit?

_____

_____

_____

_____

_____

_____

_____

_____

_____

_____

_____

_____

4. What do you think the Lord might want to say to today's church about his prayer for unity? What could we do in order to more fully live as an answer to his prayer?

_____

_____

_____

_____

_____

_____

_____

_____

_____

_____

_____

_____

Invitation and Response

God's Word always invites a response. Think about the way the theme of God's life-giving power speaks to us today. How does it invite us to respond?

The passage invites us to discover that life in God is an organic, deeply connected life in which believers draw not only nourishment but also life itself from our connection to Jesus, our source. Jesus calls us to stay connected to him and to follow the Trinity's example by thriving in unity with other believers.

What is your evaluation of yourself based on any or all of the verses found in John 14–17?

The unity of Jesus's
followers will make
the holy love of God
visible to the world.

Week Seven: Life of the Church

JOHN 20:19-21:25

Rather than think of Jesus's resurrection as the end of the gospel story, there is much to learn from studying Jesus's post-resurrection appearances. We will see Jesus's sudden and unexpected presence with the gathered disciples on the evening of that first Easter day. This powerful exchange is instructive not only in terms of the ways God enters into our experience and works to drive out fear with his love but also in terms of the commissioning that the disciples receive. A week later there is a similar appearance, now with Thomas present, which gives us the visceral interchange of doubt and faith between Thomas and Jesus. John then seems to give us the ending of the Gospel in 20:30–31, which is the statement of purpose for the narrative. But, thanks to the way the church compiled this Gospel and handed it down to us under the guidance of the Spirit, we receive a beautiful and powerful narrative of forgiveness, healing, restoration, and mission that centers on the relationship between Jesus and Peter. These final stories amount to much more than a tidy way to wrap up loose ends and bring the narrative to a close—they form a text that is meant to inform and shape the identity and nature of the church as we continue following our resurrected Lord.

WEEK 7, DAY 1

Listen to the story in John 20:19–21:25 by reading it aloud several times until you become familiar with its verses, words, and phrases. Enjoy the experience of imagining the story in your mind, picturing each event as it unfolds.

WEEK 7, DAY 2

JOHN 20:19-21:25

The Setting

In these final passages of John's Gospel, our focal point remains on John's unique theological interests in his telling of Jesus's story. The center of the Gospel narrative unfolded in chapters 18, 19, and through the first 18 verses of chapter 20 with John's version of Jesus's arrest, trials, suffering, crucifixion, death, burial, and resurrection. For our purpose this week, we want to consider how the disciples and first followers of Jesus responded to the good news of resurrection.

The Plot

To discover the plot of John 20:19–21:25, let's divide the passage into seven sections. **Below, summarize or paraphrase the general message or theme of each grouping of verses (following the pattern provided for 20:19–23, 20:24–29, and 21:20–25).**

1. John 20:19–23

After Jesus's death, the disciples hide from the Jewish leaders behind locked doors. Jesus

appears to them in the room, speaks to them, and shows them his crucifixion scars.

_____

_____

2. John 20:24–29

Thomas, who was not present when Jesus appeared, says he will not believe Jesus is alive until

he sees his crucifixion scars. Later, Jesus appears inside the locked room again and shows

Thomas his scars. Thomas professes faith that Jesus is God.

_____

_____

_____

_____

3. John 20:30–31

_____

_____

_____

_____

_____

_____

_____

_____

_____

4. John 21:1–6

_____

_____

_____

_____

_____

_____

_____

_____

_____

5. John 21:7–14

_____

_____

_____

_____

_____

_____

_____

_____

_____

6. John 21:15–19

7. John 21:20–25

Peter asks Jesus about John's future, but Jesus tells Peter not to concern himself with that, since Jesus can do anything he wants with John. John confirms that his Gospel account is true, adding that Jesus did so many other things that they could fill an infinite number of books.

WEEK 7, DAY 3

What's Happening in the Story?

As we notice certain circumstances in the story, we will begin to see how they are similar to or different from the realities of our world. The story will become the lens through which we see the world in which we live today. In our study today, you may encounter words and/or phrases that are unfamiliar to you. Some of the particular words and translation choices for them have been explained in more detail in the **Word Study Notes**. If you are interested in even more help or detail, you can supplement this study with a Bible dictionary or other Bible study resource.

WORD STUDY NOTES #1

[1] This encounter with the disciples reminds us that Jesus's resurrection is not into an otherworldly existence. He was crucified, dead, and buried on the earth, and his resurrection and new life are also on the earth, even as the biblical narrative anticipates his ascension.

[2] Jesus's action here may sound strange at first, but it is deeply rooted in the story of God. It recalls how God breathes life into the first human (Genesis 2:7) and gives life to dry bones (Ezekiel 37). Additionally, the words used for "breath" and "wind" in the Bible—pneuma—are also used for the Spirit. Thus, Jesus's breath signals the new creation as the Spirit animates the body of Christ that is sent into the world to continue the work Jesus will accomplish through them.

1. John 20:19-23

On the evening of the first Easter Day, the disciples are gathered in fear, no doubt thinking that what happened to their teacher could soon happen to them. They received Mary Magdalene's report of her encounter with the risen Lord in verse 18, but clearly, they have largely dismissed her account. They cower behind locked doors, which only makes Jesus's sudden entrance all the more dramatic as he breaks the tension and anxiety of the moment with the words, "Peace be with you!" Jesus does not scold them for their fear or embarrass them for trying to hide. He first verifies his identity by showing them the wounds in his hands and side, which seems to be the key to helping the disciples realize that he really is the Lord.[1] Jesus repeats his greeting of peace and commissions the disciples to continue in the work that the Father sent him to do. Then Jesus breathes on them.[2] Jesus's next words about forgiving sins can be challenging to interpret, but in this context they seem to indicate that his disciples, in the power of the Spirit, have the opportunity to name what God wants to do in the lives of people and in the life of the world: to forgive, redeem, and make new.

2. John 20:24–29

Here we see the well-known but perhaps often misunderstood interaction between Jesus and Thomas. John sets the stage for this encounter by noting that Thomas was not with the disciples when Jesus appeared to them before. The disciples give him the same witness they received from Mary Magdalene. This sets the stage for the second appearance of the risen Jesus, which John says occurs a week later and evidently in the same location as the first. John does not try to explain how the risen Lord suddenly appears in their midst, but in mentioning the locked doors, he emphasizes that it was not through normal means. After Jesus greets everyone again, the narrative narrows to just Jesus and Thomas.[1] Jesus does not shame Thomas but offers him exactly what he needs in order to believe. This revelation prompts perhaps the most explicit and powerful faith confession in the Gospel: "My Lord and my God!" With these words, Thomas is confessing his belief not only that Jesus is alive but also that Jesus is God.[2]

3. John 20:30–31

The powerful story ends with a blessing that Jesus offers to all who believe in him without the benefit that these first disciples enjoyed. John then turns directly to us, the readers of his Gospel, to give us what seems to be a concluding statement. Having seen the signs and wonders through John's account, we too may believe and have life in Jesus's name.

Practice the above pattern to summarize the world and reality that are portrayed in verses John 21:1-6, 7–14, 15–19, and 20–25.

WORD STUDY NOTES #2

[1] Thomas has often been saddled with the nickname "Doubting Thomas," which comes from Jesus's admonition in verse 27. However, the Greek word here is not the normal word for doubt. The Greek is apistos, which means "unbelieving." Thomas's reaction to verbal witness is really no different from the other disciples, who did not seem to believe Mary's witness until Jesus appeared to them.

[2] This confession of Jesus's divinity takes us back to what Jesus told Thomas in 14:7—that if he knows Jesus, he will know the Father. Furthermore, it takes us back to the Gospel's profound opening statement: "the Word was with God, and the Word was God" (1:1).

115

WORD STUDY NOTES #4

[1] Commentators have varying views on why the disciples return to Galilee and their fishing work. Some think it represents their failure to keep the faith and continue the mission. Regardless of our interpretation, it is clear that they have returned to what is familiar, yet without success. Perhaps John means to demonstrate that Jesus will enable them to do what they cannot accomplish on their own.

[2] The word John uses to describe the disciples' haul is the same as the word used in 6:44, when Jesus says, "No one can come to me unless the Father who sent me draws them," and in 12:32, when Jesus says, "When I am lifted up from the earth, [I] will draw all people to myself." This language suggests that the disciples now share in Jesus's work.

WORD STUDY NOTES #5

[1] Jesus presiding over the meal on the shore recalls the feeding of the multitude, his Eucharistic actions at the final meal with his disciples, and the resurrection-day meal that Luke reports in Luke 24.

4. John 21:1–6[1, 2]

5. John 21:7–14[1]

6. John 21:15–19[1, 2, 3]

_____

_____

_____

_____

_____

_____

_____

_____

_____

_____

_____

_____

7. John 21:20–25[1, 2]

_____

_____

_____

_____

_____

_____

_____

_____

_____

_____

_____

WORD STUDY NOTES #6

[1] Here, Jesus changes the metaphor from fishing to tending sheep, thereby connecting Peter's future responsibilities to Jesus's own identity as the shepherd of the sheep (see John 10).

[2] John uses two words here that are translated as "love": agape and phileo. John uses these words interchangeably throughout his Gospel. Some commentators have tried to make something of the varied uses in this passage, but perhaps the more important point is the parallel between Jesus's threefold questioning and Peter's threefold denial during Jesus's arrest and trial.

[3] Though Peter is initially hurt by Jesus's questioning, Jesus is showing him how to be faithful. Jesus seems to know that Peter's faithfulness will be tested again, next time with his life. Church tradition tells us that Peter did indeed "stretch out [his] hands" as a Christian martyr.

WORD STUDY NOTES #7

[1] Peter will be faithful in following Jesus, but his question, "What about him?" gives us an almost comical reminder of his continuing human foibles.

[2] In verses 22-23, John points out that Jesus is essentially saying to Peter, "It is not for you to worry about the fate of anyone else—only to be faithful to follow me."

Discoveries

Let's summarize some of our discoveries from John 20–21.

1. Jesus appeared to the disciples where they hid, gave them a greeting of peace, and gave them proof of his resurrection before commissioning them to continue the work the Father had sent him to do.

2. Thomas, who was not present the first time Jesus appeared, needed proof before he would believe that Jesus had risen from the dead. Jesus appeared to them again and gave Thomas all the proof he needed. Thomas then confessed his faith that Jesus was God.

3. The disciples attempted to return to their old lives as fishermen without much success. Once again, Jesus appeared to them where they were—he provided them with a miraculous catch that proved his identity to them.

4. Jesus gave Peter the opportunity to redeem his threefold denial and commissioned him to care for his followers, even to the point of death.

WEEK 7, DAY 4

The Life of the Church and the Story of God

Whenever we read a biblical text, it is important to ask how it relates to the rest of the Bible. **In the space given below, write a short summary of how the theme of God empowering people to do his work is discussed in each passage.**

1. Exodus 15:2

_____

_____

_____

_____

_____

_____

_____

_____

_____

2. Deuteronomy 31:6

_____

_____

_____

_____

_____

_____

_____

_____

_____

_____

If you have a study Bible, it may have references in a margin, a middle column, or footnotes that point to other biblical texts. You may find it helpful in understanding how the whole story of God ties together to look up some of those other scriptures from time to time.

3. Isaiah 40:29–31

4. Matthew 28:18–20

5. 2 Corinthians 12:9–10

_____

_____

_____

_____

_____

_____

_____

_____

_____

_____

_____

_____

_____

_____

6. Philippians 4:11–13

_____

_____

_____

_____

_____

_____

_____

_____

_____

_____

_____

_____

_____

WEEK 7, DAY 5

John and Our World Today

When we enter into the intriguing narrative of John 20:19 — 21:25, the story becomes the lens through which we see ourselves, our world, and God's action in our world today.

1. Of all the things Jesus might have said to his disciples at their reunion, why was "Peace be with you" the most important?

The disciples were living in fear and anxiety, hiding from those who threatened their lives.

With his greeting of peace, Jesus indicated to them what his resurrection meant—that they no

longer needed to fear and that the peace he promised them in chapter 14 was a reality.

Following the above example, answer these questions about how we understand ourselves, our world, and God's action in our world today.

2. What does Jesus's response to Thomas teach us about how to engage with our friends and loved ones who do not yet believe?

3. Has the Lord ever given you instructions that didn't seem to make a lot of sense? How might you grow in your responsiveness to his direction?

_____

_____

_____

_____

_____

_____

_____

_____

_____

_____

_____

_____

_____

4. In what ways might Jesus be calling you to a new sense of identity or purpose as you follow him? How open are you to this possibility?

_____

_____

_____

_____

_____

_____

_____

_____

_____

_____

_____

_____

_____

Invitation and Response

God's Word always invites a response. Think about the way the story of Jesus's appearances to the disciples speak to us today. How do they invite us to respond?

These stories invite us to rejoice in the reality that Jesus is alive and makes himself known

to us, even when we have trouble believing or fall back into fearful habits. Jesus's words

to Peter also call us to carry on God's mission in the world.

_____

_____

What is your evaluation of yourself based on any or all of the verses found in John 20:19 – 21:25?

_____

_____

_____

_____

_____

_____

_____

_____

_____

_____

_____

_____

_____

_____

_____

_____

_____

_____

_____

Jesus's words to Peter also call us to carry on God's mission in the world.